BAR APOCALYPSE

Matt Lyle

BROADWAY PLAY PUBLISHING INC
224 E 62nd St, NY, NY 10065
www.broadwayplaypub.com
info@broadwayplaypub.com

BARBECUE APOCALYPSE
© Copyright 2016 by Matt Lyle

Cover art by Kelly Allen

I S B N: 978-0-88145-685-1
First printing: November 2016

Book design: Marie Donovan
Page make-up: Adobe InDesign
Typeface: Palatino
Printed and bound in the U S A

BARBECUE APOCALPSE received its world premiere on 23 May 2014 at Kitchen Dog Theater (Christopher Carlos & Tina Parker, Artistic Directors; Sonya F Jones, Managing Director) in Dallas, TX. The cast and creative contributors were:

DEB...Martha Harms
MIKE .... Michael Federico
WIN...Max Hartman
ASH ....Jeff Swearingen
LULU .... Leah Spillman
GLORY...Miranda Parham
JOHN ....Barry Nash
FEMALE VOICE 1 .... Tina Parker
FEMALE VOICE 2 ....Christie Vela

Director..Lee Trull
Set designer..Michael B. Raiford
Lighting designer ....Lisa Miller
Costume/props designer..................... Samantha "Rat" Rios
Stage manager... Sarah Duc

CHARACTERS & SETTING

DEB, *co-host of the barbecues; 30s*
MIKE, *co-host of the barbecues, DEB's husband; a writer 30s*
WIN, *a handsome asshole; 30s*
ASH, *a mix between a yuppy and a hipster; 30s*
LULU, *another Yupster, ASH's wife; 30s*
GLORY, *WIN's beautiful young girlfriend, and actress/dancer; early 20s*
JOHN, *a stranger; 30s–50s*
Female Voice 1
Female Voice 2

ACT ONE: *A backyard barbecue*
ACT TWO: *A post-apocalyptic backyard barbecue one year later*

PRODUCTION NOTES

The play can be set in your state if you'd like. In the second act there is a joke at the expense of Louisiana ("I don't want to live in Louisiana!") because the play premiered in Texas. Please feel free to change any mention of Louisiana to one of your neighboring states that you feel your audience would enjoy ribbing.

ACKNOWLEDGMENTS

I cannot express enough gratitude to Kitchen Dog Theater and Lee Trull for knowing exactly what I was thinking, or to Kim, Youle, Evan, Matt, and Butch for helping me through the woods.

For Kim,
who does all the raccoon stabbing for our family.

ACT ONE

(Lights up on a beautiful raised deck and the back sliding door of a not so beautiful house. On the deck is a gas grill, a few mismatched lawn chairs, a wicker table, and some potted plants that seem to be struggling for life. We can hear a lawn being mowed and then the sound stops. We hear the mower try to restart several times. Deb enters with a tray of empty daiquiri glasses. She's wearing a white shirt, Capri pants, and a kerchief around her neck. She sets the tray down on the railing of the deck and looks toward the lawn. We hear her husband, Mike, try to start the lawn mower again and fail.)

MIKE: *(Off)* Son of a damn bitch!

DEB: What? What's wrong?

(Mike enters up the steps from the lawn. He's wearing a T-shirt and shorts.)

MIKE: It won't start.

DEB: You were just mowing.

MIKE: And now it won't start. It just died.

DEB: They are going to be here, like now and…that's a half mowed lawn. That lawn is half mowed!

MIKE: The mower died.

DEB: What do you mean it died?

MIKE: It stopped working.

DEB: Did you try to restart it?

MIKE: Like, twenty times.

DEB: Did you?

MIKE: Yes.

DEB: You pulled the thingy?

MIKE: I pulled the thingy until I couldn't pull the thingy anymore—

DEB: Do you want me to try— *(She starts backing towards the lawn.)*

MIKE: No. Deb, I swear if it—

(DEB rushes off the porch.)

MIKE: Deb! *(He looks to the sky.)* Please, God, don't let it start for her.

(We hear DEB trying to start the mower.)

MIKE: *(Loudly to DEB)* Why did we make this a barbecue anyway? I don't grill. I never grill and suddenly we have to buy this thing and it's a barbecue instead of a dinner party and then I'm grilling for six people.

(DEB re-enters.)

DEB: It won't start.

MIKE: Awe, shoot.

DEB: It's out of gas. Do we have any gas?

MIKE: No.

DEB: Shit!

MIKE: I could have done it yesterday if I'd known—

DEB: I know, I'm sorry.

MIKE: Why is it a barbecue now?

DEB: Expectations, Mike.

MIKE: Expectations?

DEB: Lowering expectations.

MIKE: Ah.

DEB: People don't expect much from a barbecue except some drinks, some charred meat, a nice deck and a fully mowed lawn! Could we syphon some gas from the car somehow?

MIKE: Who are we, the A-Team?

DEB: It looks stupid. *(She starts angrily arranging and rearranging the lawn furniture.)*

MIKE: I cannot be blamed—

DEB: It's not you—

MIKE: Don't blame—

DEB: No—

MIKE: —me—

DEB: I'm not—

MIKE: You are—

DEB: I'm not blaming—

MIKE: Better not—

DEB: I'M NOT! I LOVE YOU! *(Beat. Contrite)* I'm sorry. I'm—I'm sorry, honey. I'm sorry I'm like this and I'm sorry I'm throwing this grilling at you but why don't we have at LEAST TWO PIECES OF LAWN FURNITURE THAT MATCH?! Grownups have lawn furniture and fully mowed lawns!

MIKE: Hey, honey. Slow down. It's O K.

DEB: I know. It's fine—

MIKE: They're our friends.

DEB: I know. But Ash and Lulu are…they're Foodies—

MIKE: I know—

DEB: I can't cook for them. I was at the grocery store yesterday and started thinking about the last dinner party they had with the quail and grilled salad thing—

MIKE: It was awesome—

DEB: I know!

MIKE: Who grills salad—

DEB: But it totally worked—

MIKE: I know.

DEB: So, I was thinking about cooking for them and I started getting the flop sweats in the produce aisle. They had to have a boy come around and mop up after me—

MIKE: —Oh, honey—

DEB: —then I got home and started looking at our place and our walls—

MIKE: —No, now—

DEB: —and our "art" and our furniture—

MIKE: It's not that bad.

DEB: We're in our thirties and we have movie posters thumb-tacked on the wall. We never grew up—

MIKE: —O K, alright. We grew up—

DEB: We're kids.

MIKE: That's stupid. We grew up!

DEB: No.

MIKE: We're as adult as anyone—

DEB: We still have a stupid bean bag chair with duct tape holding in the stuffing!

MIKE: Well, where else am I going to sit when I'm playing video games?! *(Beat)* We never grew up. Why didn't we grow up?

DEB: I don't know.

MIKE: They're place is unbelievable. It's lousy with taste.

DEB: We have no style, Mike.

MIKE: Right.

DEB: They're on Apartment Therapy, like every month.

MIKE: You keep saying that and I keep meaning to ask what that means.

DEB: It's a web-site. It shows the coolest, hippest, awesomest apartments in like, America, and our friends are, like, staples. They check in with them every time the season changes to see what Ash and Lulu are doing with their place. They are interior design trendsetters and genius chefs and neither of those things are either of their jobs which are also impressive and well paying.

MIKE: I hate people that are good at things.

DEB: God, me, too. No. I like them but…I— It just makes me feel bad about myself.

MIKE: So, you panicked and changed the dinner party to a barbecue to keep them outside and so you don't have to cook.

DEB: Exactly.

MIKE: But, I can't grill, honey. I don't grill.

DEB: See, but I don't care what they think about your grilling.

MIKE: That's nefarious.

DEB: That's right. And anyway, it's steaks. You just put them on the stupid fire. The real problem is getting our guests through our house and back here before they see our shame.

MIKE: And then getting them not to notice the lawn.

DEB: We'll apologize for the lawn.

MIKE: I'll make up a joke about it.

DEB: Like what?

MIKE: Like… *(Pause)* Something funny.

DEB: Something self deprecating.

MIKE: Yes. Self-deprecate before they can deprecate.

DEB: One. Two. Three.

DEB & MIKE: Go Team.

(MIKE starts examining the grill.)

MIKE: They've seen our house before.

DEB: Once.

MIKE: That's it?

DEB: When we moved in and they talked about how much potential it had.

MIKE: Oh, yeah.

DEB: We have aborted that potential.

MIKE: Yeah. We suck.

DEB: We do.

(Pause)

MIKE: I love you, anyway.

DEB: I love you, in spite of it all. This deck is our prized possession.

MIKE: It is very nice.

DEB: You are quite the carpenter and the barbecue will show that off.

MIKE: *(A little sad)* I had no idea I could do something like this. Maybe that's what I should have done with my life. You know? I shoulda been a carpenter— *(Regarding the grill)* So, you turn the knobs— Can I tell you I'm kind of afraid of this thing? What if it explodes?

DEB: It won't explode. Will it?

MIKE: Probably not.

DEB: You need me to light it?

MIKE: No, I don't need you to light it.

DEB: O K.

MIKE: Maybe I'll trick Win into lighting it. He'll love that I don't know how to grill.

DEB: Win. God. I was stressing so much about Ash and Lulu I forgot about him and, the girl. What's her name? What's her name!?

MIKE: Umm… Triumph, I think? Is that right?

DEB: No—

MIKE: Victory? Wonder Woman?

DEB: Something like that. Success—

MIKE: Sexy.

(Beat. DEB has stopped MIKE with a look.)

MIKE: We were naming her with superlatives. Victory… Success…

DEB: I know, she's young and beautiful. I know that.

MIKE: I swear he could have any woman he wants.

DEB: I don't know about that.

MIKE: C'mon. He's a freaking triathlete business tycoon.

DEB: He's a triathlete business dildo.

MIKE: Well… yeah—

DEB: Why do we always have to invite him to stuff?

MIKE: We've known each other for a long time. We're friends.

DEB: You're friends with a guy that you admit is a jerk—

MIKE: Mm, yes—

DEB: —and treats you poorly—

MIKE: Uh, huh—

DEB: He lives to make fun of you, right? Right?

MIKE: If by "lives to make fun of me" you mean that he makes fun of me all of the time and really enjoys it, then yes, I guess so.

DEB: Why?

MIKE: I don't know. That's our relationship. Men bust each other's balls.

DEB: You never bust back.

MIKE: I guess his balls aren't as bustable as my balls are.

DEB: Oh, his balls are bustable and today, if he starts in on your balls in front of Ash and Lulu I want you to bust his balls right back.

MIKE: I'll try.

DEB: If you don't bust his balls I'll bust his balls for you.

MIKE: This is sounding gross—

DEB: —Mike.

MIKE: I'll bust his balls until they explode everywhere, O K?

DEB: Awwe. Good. I love you, honey.

MIKE: I love you.

DEB: If you don't fight back it's just him being mean to you. Not playful banter. You are a big man.

MIKE: Ha.

DEB: You're my big man. You're my sweet tater big man. You built this deck. You're published.

MIKE: Yeah.

DEB: Don't roll your stupid eyes.

MIKE: It was a short story.

DEB: So?

MIKE: I got fifty dollars for it.

DEB: So!?

MIKE: So, that doesn't qualify.

DEB: As what? It's a success. It's not the great American novel but somebody paid you for something you wrote—

MIKE: —O K, O K—

DEB: —you are a professional writer.

MIKE: O K.

DEB: Why can't you enjoy that?

MIKE: Because.

DEB: You drive me crazy.

MIKE: Don't get mad.

DEB: I'm not, but it was an accomplishment. Just admit it.

MIKE: You're mad.

DEB: I'm not mad. I'm not. I just want you to stop beating yourself up and admit it was a FUCKING ACCOMPLISHMENT! God, you make me mad!

MIKE: It was an accomplishment! It was. I can make a third of a payment on my student loans.

DEB: Damn it, Mike.

MIKE: No. O K. I know. You're right. I know. I'm, you know, learning that I don't need recognition or monetary compensation for my work. I just find the work itself rewarding.

DEB: That is so…healthy—

MIKE: I was being facetious—

DEB: Damnit.

MIKE: Sarcasm.

DEB: Mike—

MIKE: I can't tell people I'm a writer if I'm in my thirties, work at a digital photo lab, have been published once in a bad magazine that no one likes, and only have fifty dollars to show for a creative writing degree. Get where I'm coming from?

DEB: Well—

MIKE: So, please, please, please don't mention the story. I'm just not that proud of it and it makes it awkward for me. O K? Please?

DEB: O K. I promise.

MIKE: Good. It's five o'clock.

DEB: *(Freaked out)* AH! I need—I've still got stuff to do inside!

MIKE: Need help?

DEB: No. Put the mower up. Oh, and water the plants.

Deb starts to go inside.

MIKE: Which ones?

DEB: The plants.

MIKE: Which plants?

DEB: *(Gesturing to all of the plants)* The ones right here.

MIKE: How much water?

DEB: What? I don't know. Some.

MIKE: Aren't they all different? Don't they take different amounts at, like, different times?

DEB: Well…

MIKE: When was the last time you watered—

DEB: Do you want to take over plant care?

MIKE: Well, no—

DEB: Then just water the stupid plants and put the mower away.

MIKE: O K. O K.

(DEB *starts to go inside again.*)

MIKE: Hey, honey. What's with the…the…

(MIKE*'s gesturing about the kerchief around* DEB*'s neck. She gasps.*)

DEB: Does it look stupid?

MIKE: No!

DEB: I just wanted to accessorize!

MIKE: It's cute!

DEB: It's stupid!

MIKE: It's not!

DEB: I just don't have any jewelry or any cute, hip clothes and I don't have a face for hats so I saw this and thought it would look Italian maybe. Do I look like Sophia Loren or Fred from Scooby Doo?

MIKE: Well—

(DEB *takes it off.*)

DEB: I'm Fred from Scooby Doo.

(DEB *throws the kerchief at* MIKE *and exits.*)

MIKE: You don't look like Fred!

(DEB's *gone*.)

MIKE: *(Quietly)* Jinkies.

(MIKE *wipes his face and neck with the kerchief and goes to water the plants. While his back is turned,* WIN, *all Aviators and bronzer, enters carrying a six pack of beer. He sneaks up on* MIKE, *grabs him from behind and feigns cutting his throat*.)

MIKE: Oh, shit!

WIN: Boom. That's how it goes. I sneak up on you, I cut your throat then take everything you own. Your life, your woman, your old busted lawn chairs. Then I melt back into the forest like a ghost.

MIKE: Nice to see you, Win.

WIN: You didn't hear me coming?

MIKE: No.

WIN: You have no primitive instincts. You've been completely softened by society.

MIKE: You own a tanning bed. *(He has gone back to watering the plants.)*

WIN: What are you doing?

MIKE: *(Beat)* I seem to be watering plants.

WIN: No. That's Southern Maidenhair and you're just pouring cold water in the soil? In the spring you're supposed to mist the whole plant with warm water.

MIKE: I knew it.

WIN: And where's your fucking gravel in the drain dish? You've got to keep the humidity high. Are you a moron?

MIKE: Kinda.

WIN: *(Noticing another plant)* Jesus, man, what are you people doing to this Goosefoot?

MIKE: Goosefoot?

WIN: Goosefoot grows for anybody. Like, it's a great gift for retarded people, and this one— It's like if a plant could get rickets, that's what it would look like.

MIKE: That sounds about right.

WIN: God bless your future damaged children.

MIKE: The goosefoot is the last straw. No kids.

WIN: Really? No procreation? Not gonna spread your seed?

MIKE: Oh, I don't know.

WIN: You guys having trouble? Is there trouble?

MIKE: What? No, things are fine.

WIN: Fine?

MIKE: Yeah, fine. We've been married a long time and things are, you know, fine.

WIN: Well, that sounds fine. Man, you gotta stop living fine and live big.

MIKE: I'm within my rights to use the word "fine" in a positive way.

WIN: Was everything just "Fine" between Antony and Cleopatra?

MIKE: She committed suicide by snake.

WIN: That's a bad—

MIKE: Terrible—

WIN: That's a terrible example but you have to aim higher, man. You can't shrug, "Oh, things are fine, fine, I'll just pick my nose. That'll be fine." You're a medium.

MIKE: I'm a…

WIN: A medium.

MIKE: Uh, huh. I talk to dead people?

WIN: Like small, medium, large. I'm a large. You're medium. Like, homeless people are smalls. I might be a extra-large.

MIKE: Win—

WIN: Go big or go home, Mike. You gotta live by that.

MIKE: I already live by go big or go incrementally smaller…based on the appropriateness of how big circumstances suggest I go—

WIN: I am trying to help you, ass. If something you want presents itself what do you do? You pussy think about it. You weigh your pussy options. You look at it from both pussy sides and then you do something pussy safe and everything is pussy fine. Something I want presents itself and I punch it in the dick, throw it over my shoulder, laugh all the way home.

MIKE: You're mixing your genital metaphors again.

WIN: I'm a business man, Mike. I do business. I make deals with the most powerful people in this city on a daily basis. A daily fucking basis, Mike. You know what I'm saying?

MIKE: You're saying you're a business man.

WIN: No room for compromise. Cut throat. All I can worry about is my six figures. Fuck everybody else. You've got to get Ayn Rand on this bitch. Get it?

MIKE: I never read *Atlas Shrugged*—

WIN: Me either but that doesn't mean it's not true. Confidence, Mike. You've got no confidence. That's why you're okay with things being fine. I've got confidence that I could have anything I want so I end up getting it. You know what I'm saying?

MIKE: You're saying that I suck.

WIN: No. Well, basically. Beer?

MIKE: Yeah. There should be room in the cooler.

(WIN tosses MIKE a beer, takes one for himself and goes to the cooler.)

WIN: I really am just trying to help you.

MIKE: And I sincerely appreciate it.

WIN: I like beer.

MIKE: Me, too. So…so, how's living big with…um… wonder wom—

WIN: Glory. Her name is Glory and it's awesome. Mind blowingly incredible. She's crazy about me and sex, oh my God. Things got so cray cray the other night I almost called the cops on us.

MIKE: Wow.

WIN: It's like the sky opens and a shaft of heavenly fire shoots down right on my wiener.

MIKE: *(He means it.)* That sounds like fun.

WIN: It'll put hair on your chest.

MIKE: Where is she?

WIN: She'll be late. She's got an audition. Get this, to be a Rockette.

MIKE: Really?

WIN: You know what that means?

MIKE: She might be a Rockette—

WIN: I could be fucking a Rockette, Mike.

MIKE: I'll add it to my prayer list.

WIN: C'mon. You wouldn't want to?

MIKE: I'm married.

WIN: Mike. Look at me. Look into my hazel eyes. Wouldn't you like to be able to defile a Rockette?

MIKE: Would I like to…

WIN: Defile. Defile, Mike. They're in peak physical condition to do all those kicks. They're bendy. Be honest.

MIKE: Yeah, I guess I would.

WIN: Fuckinay you would. You remember in High School when I was quarterback and dating all the cheerleaders?

MIKE: I remember. I was dating them, too… in my mind.

WIN: Well, life is better now. This one might be the one. Like, besides all the stuff I do to her, I think I might love her, too.

(DEB *enters from the house. She's wearing a completely different outfit.*)

DEB: Mike! For the love of God, the lawn-mower!

MIKE: *(Beat. Then running off. Sarcastic)* AHHH!

DEB: Dork.

WIN: Hello, Deb.

DEB: Oh, Jesus. Hi, Win.

WIN: Thanks for having me.

DEB: Oh, no problem. Where's…

WIN: Glory. We broke up.

DEB: Really?

WIN: No. You shoulda seen your face. She'll be here in a minute. She's auditioning to be a Rockette.

DEB: Wow. A Rockette? That's impressive.

WIN: Yes, it is.

DEB: Have you ever seen a Rockettes show?

WIN: Oh, god no. But still. You look good.

DEB: Please don't.

WIN: Real good.

(Pause)

DEB: Fuck you, Win.

WIN: And Mike's abusing your plants.

DEB: What?

WIN: He's just watering indiscriminately with no regard for variety.

DEB: Oh…Mike. I told him, but, you know him…

(We can hear a car pull up.)

DEB: I hear a car! *(She rushes in. Beat. She sticks her head out.)* MIKE! They're here!

WIN: Whoa.

(MIKE rushes on screaming in mock panic and then back off again.)

WIN: Dude, your lawn has a mohawk.

MIKE: *(Off)* It's rebelling.

(WIN laughs.)

WIN: Rebelling. Ha!

(MIKE re-enters.)

MIKE: That was pretty funny, huh? Do you mind saying that again when Ash and Lulu get here? Deb wants us to be charmingly self deprecating about the lawn and I've been trying to think of a joke but that's a good one.

WIN: Yeah, I'll say it. What's with Deb? She seems nervous.

MIKE: She's a little apprehensive.

WIN: She's a little insane.

MIKE: It's Ash and Lulu. They make her feel inadequate or something.

WIN: She's like ten times hotter than Lu.

MIKE: I don't think hotness is—

WIN: And Ash, I swear that guy is wearing panties under his chinos. You know, I can't figure out if they're hipsters or yuppies. They're yupsters.

MIKE: That's not nice. It's accurate, but it's not nice.

(ASH *and* LULU *enter through the fence's side gate. It doesn't open all of the way so it's a little bit of a struggle. They're being practically pushed by* DEB. ASH *is buried in his iPhone.*)

DEB: Oh, yeah—

LULU: Ow—

DEB: Sorry— Yeah, it's a little broken, but, but this way you can see the deck. And here we are! Mike's awesome deck. He built it himself.

ASH: Wow!

DEB: He's like a real carpenter. I have no idea what we did before he built it. We use it all of the time. Barbecuing and breakfast-breakfast-breakfast-brunch, just relaxing—it's so relaxing and nice. So nice. We never like, well, it's so nice to eat outside, we just do it all of the time, just all the time…and Mike had a story published!

ASH: Congrats!

LULU: Nice!

DEB: Yay! In a very prestigious journal and he got paid…very well and so everything is just great. Just great. He's a real writer and a carpenter.

(Beat)

MIKE: Hi, guys!

ASH: Hey, man. Look—

(ASH puts his phone in MIKE's face.)

MIKE: Nice…phone.

ASH: Thanks, but see— It's your house from space. It's the new satellite App.

(They look up. ASH waves at the sky.)

DEB: Let me see. Wow. That's amazing. Mike, don't you think that's amazing? What a phone. I should get one. We should get one, Mike.

ASH: Well, two. You'd need two. We both have one.

LULU: I don't use mine much.

(Beat)

MIKE: Lu!

LULU: Mike!

(They hug.)

LULU: Thanks for having us.

MIKE: No problem.

DEB: We should have you guys over more, I know. Things get hectic—

LULU: Yeah, and life—

DEB: Just busy. So busy.

ASH: Hey, Win.

WIN: Hay's for horses but then so is having a big dick sooo…I'll take it.

MIKE: *(Beat)* O K. *(To ASH)* What'd you guys bring?

ASH: Oh, it's meat.

MIKE: Meat?

LULU: Yeah, we're only eating organic beef now so we thought we'd bring some.

MIKE: Oh, I got—I think what I got said it was all natural.

LULU: Yeah, that's not the same. No, yeah, no. Anybody can say their meat is all natural because "all natural" hasn't been defined by the F D A.

ASH: It means whatever the food companies want it to mean.

LULU: But "organic" refers to food grown without synthetic pesticides, insecticides, herbicides, fungicides, hormones, fertilizers or other synthetic or toxic substances.

ASH: Antibiotics.

LULU: God, don't get me started on the use of antibiotics in livestock.

MIKE: We could have gotten some organic stuff.

ASH: Well, it's expensive.

MIKE: We can afford organic food.

WIN: They just don't give a shit.

MIKE: Well, there's that—

ASH: Hey, sorry—

MIKE: No, it's O K.

LULU: We just didn't want to force our organic crusade on you guys.

DEB: No, it's good. We should, you know—crusade— I've always thought I should be more, you know, conscious of, you know, what is in our food—

LULU: It's disgusting. They're poisoning us.

DEB: Exactly.

MIKE: Would anybody like a drink?

WIN: I like drinking.

MIKE: There's beer and Deb made some fruity something or other—

DEB: Mango Margarita.

ASH: Ooh, Mango Margarita please.

WIN: Ha! This guy!

DEB: Lulu?

LULU: Oh, nothing for me.

DEB: Really?

LULU: Well, do you have any ginger ale?

DEB: No.

LULU: Well, water with lemon then.

DEB: Oh. Oh! O K. *(She starts inside but stops short.)* Do you want any alcohol in that?

LULU: No, thanks.

DEB: *(Looking at* LULU's *stomach. Excited)* O K… *(She exits.)*

WIN: Mike, your yard has a Mowhawk!

(He exits into the house. LULU *and* ASH *look at the yard and* MIKE.*)*

MIKE: It's rebelling.

(Pause)

ASH: Oh. Funny.

MIKE: Thanks.

ASH: Very comical.

MIKE: Yeah, well…

ASH: Nice grill.

MIKE: Yeah. It's brand new. Do you have one?

ASH: We have charcoal. I've never used a gas grill. Honey?

LULU: No, I've always had a charcoal grill. I think charcoal gives the food a richer flavor than gas.

MIKE: Huh.

LULU: I mean gas is good, too.

ASH: Have you seen the viral video of the pigeon getting umm…asphyxiate by the fumes of a grill.

MIKE: No.

LULU: It's awesome. Somebody's filming some kids jumping rope in the foreground and you can see the grill really smoking in the background—

ASH: No, let me find it. *(He starts typing into his phone.)* You can't describe it. You just have to see it.

LULU: It's crazy. It was like the "Is this real life" kid.

MIKE: Who's that?

LULU: You haven't seen that?!

ASH: Oh, my god. Oh, my god. You have to see that. It's this high kid. I'm going to pull that up.

LULU: *(Mimicking a stoned kid)* Is this real life?

ASH: No, wait—wait for it. You can't do it justice.

LULU: Well, sorry.

ASH: I'm not getting— This is slow. Do you usually get 4G here?

MIKE: I don't know—

ASH: I feel like I had 4G when we got here but now I only have two stupid bars. C'mon!

LULU: *(Checking phone)* I only have two bars, too.

ASH: This sucks. That kid is so funny.

MIKE: So, somebody got the kid high?

LULU: He just went to the dentist—

ASH: No! Shut up. You'll ruin it. You just have to see it. It's buffering.

MIKE: It's O K—

ASH: No, it's good. We just have to wait a few— It's buffering…buffering. Buffering…buffering. C'mon… buffering. Oh! Duh. Do you have wireless!?

MIKE: Yeah.

ASH: Which one is it?

MIKE: Europenis.

ASH: You named your network Europenis?

MIKE: I did.

ASH: Funny. Very comical.

MIKE: Well, thanks.

LULU: Have you guys been to Europe?

MIKE: No.

LULU: Huh. Well, you should. We've been a few times but Ash was just there for a month with his work.

MIKE: Wow. That's awesome. I would love to go. We talk about it.

LULU: You have to go. You have to. Oh, god, the food is exquisite.

ASH: What's your password?

MIKE: Umm…dingoatedebsbaby.

ASH: Dingoatedebsbaby?

MIKE: Yeah.

ASH: Comical. Nice.

LULU: What's that?

ASH: It's from a movie.

LULU: Oh.

ASH: You've never heard that?

LULU: No.

MIKE: It was Meryl Streep as an Australian lady. *(In an Australian accent)* Dingo ate my ba—

ASH: No! Wait. I'm Youtubing it. No Vimeo. It's more elegant.

MIKE: You should Youtube how to start this grill.

ASH: You don't know how to start your grill?

MIKE: No. Do you?

(Pause. ASH *looks at the grill.)*

ASH: I'll Google it.

*(*DEB *enters quickly with a tray of drinks. She slams the door behind her. She seems a little out of sorts but quickly pulls herself back together.)*

DEB: Mango Margaritas!

ASH: Yummy!

LULU: Our husbands don't know how to start the grill.

DEB: Mike, are you still scared it might explode?

MIKE: I'm not scared—

LULU: It could explode?

DEB: Maybe.

MIKE: I mean it is combustible. It makes sense that it could explode.

LULU: Oh, my God, another reason to use charcoal.

MIKE: Uh, huh.

DEB: It's not time to eat anyway. Everyone get your drink.

ASH: This is a beautiful drink.

(ASH *puts his drink on the table and takes a picture of it with his phone and shows it to* LULU.)

ASH: Look.

LULU: I know. I can see it in real life right there.

DEB: Did you just take a picture of it with your phone?

ASH: Yep. 14 Megapixels.

DEB: Wow!

ASH: I take pictures of everything.

(WIN *enters and gets another beer.*)

DEB: Hey, let's have a toast. Get your drinks. C'mon.

ASH: Whoa! Twitter is blowing up right now—

LULU: We're trying to toast, honey. Twitter can wait a second.

DEB: O K. A toast. Thank you guys for coming over. To good friends and to great times. Let's have the best barbecue ever. Cheers.

ASH: Hear, hear.

(*They drink.*)

DEB: So, Lulu. When are you due?

(ASH *and* LULU *spit their drinks.*)

LULU: I'm not pregnant, Deb.

WIN: Oh, shit!

DEB: Oh, my god. Oh, my god.

LULU: What made you think I was?

DEB: Well, you weren't drinking.

LULU: And I'm fat. I know.

DEB: No! You're not fat! You're not!

WIN: It's just a pot belly.

LULU: I want a drink.

(She takes ASH*'s drink.)*

ASH: Honey, do you think you should—

*(*LULU *downs the drink in one long swallow.)*

WIN: Oh, shit.

*(*LULU *finishes the drink and a moment later has a massive brain freeze.)*

LULU: AHHHHH!!!!!!!! Oh, Oh, Oh. AHHH!! Too... cold. I need—I need your rest room.

DEB: Please, no—

LULU: Where is it?

DEB: It's out of order—

LULU: Deb! Please—

*(*DEB *opens the door for her.)*

LULU: Where is it?

DEB: Down the hall. Seventh door on the left. *(Pause)* That's a joke. There's only two doors. *(Pause)* Second door on the left.

*(*LULU *is gone.)*

ASH: She's fine.

MIKE: She seemed fine.

ASH: She has her mother's body type. She carries all extra weight in the front. It makes her look like she might be—

*(*ASH *and* WIN *speak together.)*

ASH: —pregnant.

WIN: A fifty year old man. Oh, I thought that's what you were going to say...

ASH: Anyway, a little five year old girl at Whole Foods yesterday asked her about the baby in her tummy.

DEB: Oh, my god.

ASH: So, it's the second one in two days.

MIKE: *(To* DEB*)* We don't have any loose poisons in the house do we?

DEB: Oh, my God.

ASH: Oh, no that's silly. *(Beat)* Well, I'll go in and check on her.

MIKE: Good idea.

ASH: *(To* MIKE*)* Hey, so I Googled "How to light gas grill" and got all of these pages.

*(*ASH *hands* MIKE *his phone.)*

MIKE: Oh, thanks.

*(*ASH *exits.)*

WIN: So…

MIKE: I know.

WIN: You don't know how to light your grill?

MIKE: Win—

WIN: The grill you own?

MIKE: Yes.

WIN: Mike, I've been meaning to ask you if you're a man?

MIKE: Yes.

WIN: Do you have a penis?

MIKE: Yes, I—

WIN: Actually a brain would do.

DEB: You guys—

WIN: Seriously, you can just add this to your list of non-accomplishments.

DEB: That is so rude.

MIKE: Deb—

DEB: For your information we are standing on one of his accomplishments.

(WIN *checks the bottom of his feet.*)

MIKE: Deb—

WIN: Oh, that's right. The deck.

MIKE: O K, Deb—

DEB: No, Mike. Win needs to hear this. This deck took him months and he worked very, very hard. He didn't always know what he was doing but he slowly, painstakingly figured it out. He hurt himself, like, thirty times. I just wanted to do it for him but he wouldn't let me. And it ended up looking amazing.

WIN: Yeah. It does look great. Nice work, man.

MIKE: Thanks.

WIN: I meant to say something earlier. Nice.

MIKE: It turned out.

WIN: It sure did.

DEB: I just don't understand this relationship.

(*We hear a car pull up.*)

DEB: Car!

She sprints off through the house.

MIKE: There she goes.

WIN: Uh, huh.

MIKE: (*Re: the grill*) So, I gotta light this thing at some point.

WIN: Want me to show you how?

MIKE: You know how?

WIN: Well, I can figure it out. (*He stares at the grill for a few seconds.*) Have you read the instructions?

MIKE: I have.

WIN: And you still don't know how to light it?

MIKE: Well, I do know. I think. In theory.

WIN: Why don't you light it?

MIKE: I'm scared.

WIN: Scared?

MIKE: Mm. Terrified.

WIN: You're terrified of your grill?

MIKE: Yes.

WIN: You're afraid…

MIKE: It will blow up.

WIN: That's stupid.

MIKE: Is it impossible?

WIN: Well, no.

MIKE: I'm not going to risk my life for a few steaks.

WIN: Do you use your oven?

MIKE: Yes.

WIN: It could blow up, too.

MIKE: Nope.

WIN: Why not?

MIKE: All electric. I think you turn this and push this—

(MIKE *pushes the button. They both flinch, but it doesn't light.* ASH *coaxes* LULU *out. We get the vague sense of someone calling a dog.*)

ASH: C'mon out. Lu— Lulu. C'mon out.

LULU: Mike, how can you cook on an electric stove?

MIKE: I don't know how to answer that question.

ASH: Got my phone?

MIKE: Yeah.

ASH: It's like one of my appendages.

LULU: Except it always works.

WIN: Nice dick joke.

LULU: Hey, Mike! Movie posters! You got movie posters in there! Ash, we should get some old, like French movie posters to re-decorate our garage.

MIKE: RE-decorate your garage?

ASH: Oh, yeah. I love that idea. The style of old, French movies is just totally mint.

WIN: You guys like French films?

ASH: Oh, no. Just the posters.

LULU: Hey, you guys got any Tuaca?

MIKE: I don't know.

LULU: How could you not know what's in your house?

MIKE: Deb kind of keeps up with what we have…and where things go.

WIN: Hey, Ashley—

ASH: I prefer Ash.

LULU: He is an Ashley, though.

WIN: Tired of people thinking you're a woman?

ASH: In writing. People think I'm a woman in writing. The name coupled with my penmanship…

WIN: I thought it might be the skinny jeans.

ASH: Very comical.

LULU: It was. It was very funny.

WIN: *(Beat)* Mike's scared of the grill.

MIKE: They're scared of it, too.

WIN: Really?

(ASH *and* LULU *nod.)*

LULU: Yup.

ASH: Terrified.

(DEB *and* GLORY *enter through the gate on the fence to the side of the deck. It doesn't open all of the way so it's a mighty struggle to get through.*)

DEB: We're all out back already. It doesn't open all the—

(DEB *has made it through.* GLORY *squeezes through the gate.*)

DEB: Here let me help—

GLORY: I'm O K. I got it—

DEB: Sort of squat—

GLORY: I'm good. I'm good. I'm caught. I'm caught.

DEB: Here—

GLORY: No.

DEB: Here—

GLORY: I got it.

DEB: Let me—

(GLORY *finally squeezes through. Her dress gets caught on the fence and rips.*)

GLORY: Oh!

DEB: Oh! No!

GLORY: It ripped.

DEB: I'm so sorry.

GLORY: It's O K.

DEB: No, I'm sorry! Are you O K?

GLORY: I'm fine. My audition dress on the other hand—

DEB: I can sew it.

GLORY: You sew?

DEB: Well, no.

GLORY: It's fine.

DEB: I can learn how.

GLORY: It's fine. I'm not naked.

WIN: And that's a goddamn shame!

GLORY: Win! Baby!

WIN: Get that sweet ass up here! Get it up here!

DEB: Here let me help—

GLORY: Please—

(DEB *helps* GLORY *up on the deck and through the railing.*)

MIKE: Deb—

GLORY: Ouch—

DEB: Just put your leg up—

(GLORY *makes it onto the deck.* DEB *starts to climb up.*)

DEB: I'll…just—

MIKE: Honey, honey—

DEB: —join you. I'm not as flexible as I ow—

MIKE: Deb—

DEB: Mike! What?

MIKE: Why don't you take the stairs?

(*Pause.* DEB *gets back on the ground. Everyone watches her walk to the stairs and up them. She stops at the top.*)

DEB: I forgot they were there.

(GLORY *and* WIN *kiss each other lustily.*)

WIN: Baby, I missed you.

GLORY: Oh, baby.

LULU: That was a loud kiss!

WIN: How was the audish?

GLORY: Nailed it! I hit every combination and the assistant choreographer said I have a beautiful kick.

WIN: Your kicks are the best.

GLORY: I know, right!?

MIKE: Do you want a beer?

GLORY: Oh, hi, Mark! No. No unnecessary carbs. I don't want a pot belly.

(LULU *moans.*)

MIKE: Glory, you remember Ash and Lulu.

GLORY: Yes. Hello!

ASH: Good to see you again.

GLORY: You, too.

LULU: Hi. I need some unnecessary carbs. (*She fishes a beer from the cooler.*)

ASH: (*Looking at his phone*) Hey, something weird is happening on twitter.

MIKE: Is it our Wifi?

ASH: No, people are saying weird stuff. There seems to be something big going on but it's not making sense.

LULU: Could you get out of your phone? Jesus. Life is out here. Life is out here.

ASH: Honey.

LULU: Turn it off.

ASH: Lulu—

LULU: Turn it off and participate fully in your physical and social life. (*She drinks half her beer. Belches*) Let's all sit down and talk with no phones. No tweeting. No goooogling. Let's just make conversation like people used to.

DEB: I agree. Everyone, have a seat and let's just relax. Let's shoot the bull.

LULU: Yeah! Let's shoot the bull—like the olden days.

MIKE: I'm gonna get this grill started if it kills me.

(MIKE *goes to the grill. Everyone else finds a seat or a place to lean.*)

DEB: So, Glory. You had an audition?

GLORY: I did. I did. For the Rockettes. Pretty exciting. I'm sure I'll get through this round at least and I kind of think this is it. I feel like it's my time.

WIN: I can't believe I'm going to be dating a Rockette!

GLORY: If I do get it I'll have to leave the show I'm in now.

DEB: Ooh, what are you in?

GLORY: I'm a dancer in *Annie Get Your Gun* starring Tom Wopat.

MIKE: Fire in the hole.

(MIKE *pushes the button. They all flinch. Nothing)*

DEB: That's awesome. We should see that. I love the theater.

MIKE: Who is Tom Wopat?

DEB: Mike—

MIKE: I feel like I recognize the name but...

(MIKE *pushes the button again. They all flinch.)*

GLORY: You don't know who Tom Wopat is?

MIKE: No?

ASH: Me either.

LULU: Me three.

GLORY: He's one of the great American musical actors. City of Angels? Guys and Dolls? Anybody? Win?

WIN: I've never heard of him.

GLORY: Really? He was in one of the *Chicago* revivals and *42nd Street*. He did *Annie Get Your Gun* with Bernadette Peters and Reba Mcentire.

MIKE: I've heard of them.

DEB: Me, too.

GLORY: I can't believe none of you know him. He's kind of a big deal.

DEB: I guess we should get to the theater more often.

MIKE: Yeah. I guess so.

(Pause. MIKE pushes the button. They all flinch.)

ASH: *(Looking at his phone)* Luke Duke!

MIKE: Oh!

DEB: Yeah!

WIN: I knew I knew the name!

LULU: Fucking Luke Duke!

GLORY: Who?

ASH: Luke Duke. *(Beat)* Tom Wopat played Luke Duke.

(Beat)

GLORY: I don't know what that is.

WIN: *The Dukes of Hazard*.

MIKE: You've never seen *The Dukes of Hazard*?

GLORY: No. Is it a musical?

MIKE: Ha. Um, no. It was an awesome T V show.

WIN: Hell, yeah.

ASH: In the eighties.

GLORY: Oh, I was born in 1991.

LULU: Holy Shit!

GLORY: What?

LULU: I had washboard abs when I was your age. Just naturally washboardy—

DEB: Lulu—

LULU: Well, I did.

WIN: She has an old soul.

LULU: And a young, bouncy ass.

WIN: You get drunk quick.

LULU: I do. I really do.

ASH: She does.

(Everyone but GLORY laughs.)

WIN: The eighties. That was a decade.

(There's a general approval from everyone but GLORY.)

WIN: I mean Ronald Reagan!

(There's a general disapproval from everyone. MIKE hits the button. Flinch)

MIKE: Damn.

WIN: Lemme tell you if Ronald Reagan was still president we'd all be rich.

MIKE: If Ronald Reagan was still the president he'd be a zombie.

DEB: He wouldn't raise taxes but he would eat our brains.

WIN: Hilarious. You wanna give all these handouts to bums—

DEB: I want to?

WIN: People like you want to give everything to everybody when you gotta take what you want and keep that shit for yourself. It's natural selection. I say fuck the homeless—

MIKE: We should fuck homeless people?

WIN: Not fuck the homeless. Fuck the homeless. And leave us job creators alone.

(A beat and then everyone else is amused to some degree.)

WIN: Are my balls being busted here?

DEB: You bet your ass.

GLORY: Cutting the top tax rate doesn't lead to wage growth.

(Beat)

WIN: What—now, honey. C'mon.

GLORY: C'mon what?

WIN: Well…you were born in the nineties.

GLORY: Well, I know that cutting the top tax rate doesn't lead to wage growth.

WIN: How?

GLORY: I played an economics person. I said that in the play. *(Acting it out)* Frankly, Mister Roosevelt, cutting the top tax rate doesn't lead to wage growth! *(She slams her fist down.)* Any economist worth their salt— Economist! That's the word. I liked that play. My costume was this amazing, sort of perfectly tailored business suit. I think if I wasn't an actress maybe I would have been an economist.

(Beat)

WIN: You are all liberals right? Of course, you are. Ash and Lulu, successful yuppies in their thirties make for middle aged Republicans.

ASH: How do you figure?

WIN: Your earning potential. You'll just keep climbing those income brackets and soon you'll be Republicans. You won't even know what happened to you.

ASH: I don't think so.

WIN: Deb is whatever Mike is because her whole identity is wrapped up with making Mike feel good about himself.

DEB: It is not.

WIN: Deb, come on. Mike published a story! Mike's a carpenter! Mike let's me know when he needs his didee changed!

LULU: I think things are getting serious.

WIN: No. We're just fucking around.

GLORY: I've never voted.

LULU: Jesus god.

WIN: Dude, I'm kidding. Mike's a great guy. You're my best friend. I'm just— You just have an artist's temperament but not the requisite skills so…it's rendered you kinda useless to society.

(Pause. MIKE *puts his head in the grill and pushes the button five times really quickly. Beat)*

ASH: I'm gonna tell everyone a funny story now. I was in *Shanghai (A very authentic pronunciation)* studying the point of purchase environment there and I bought what I thought was gum. Turns out it was actually condoms.

GLORY: Oh, no! Condoms taste terrible!

ASH: Yes, they do.

MIKE: Just because something doesn't make money, doesn't make it worthless.

WIN: Look let's drop it. I'm sorry. *(Beat)* But that is the definition of worthless.

MIKE: Glory. Win has herpes.

DEB: Yes!

LULU: Dayum!

ASH: Now that's comical!

WIN: How much did your writing gig pay?

DEB: Mike—

MIKE: Five thousand…pennies.

WIN: Fifty bucks.

GLORY: I've acted for a lot less.

LULU: I'm not drunk enough for this. And I'm pretty drunk. Deb, do you have any Tuaca?

DEB: Yes.

ASH: Lulu—

LULU: Ashley. *(To* DEB*)* Show me the Tuaca, Deb. She's going inside.

DEB: Mike, stop her.

MIKE: What?

DEB: Mike!

MIKE: O K! *(He starts to go inside and stops.)* Why do I have to—

DEB: Because I can't watch her looking at my house!

(MIKE *backs into the house.)*

DEB: I guess that sounded weird.

ASH: Nah—

GLORY: —No—

WIN: —Yes.

DEB: Sorry.

(DEB *sits down. A very awkward pause)*

GLORY: I'm going to powder my nose.

DEB: Just squat behind the bushes. *(Beat)* That sounded weird, too, huh? I'm—I'm weird. Go on in. What does it matter?

GLORY: Where…is…it?

DEB: I don't know.

ASH: Umm, turn left after the bean bag—

DEB: Jesus.

ASH: You know what, I'll show you.

GLORY: Thanks.

(They go inside. Pause)

WIN: You know what you need? A real man. You wouldn't be so fucking neurotic—

DEB: Win—

WIN: Seriously. You'd have the house of your dreams. Stainless. Granite. People like Ashley and PooPoo couldn't make you feel inadequate. You could be proud of your husband.

DEB: Shut up—

(WIN's getting closer to DEB.)

WIN: Now, you slapped the shit out of me inside and I forgive you.

DEB: Win, you stay away—

WIN: That's not what you want—

DEB: Yes, it is—

(WIN grabs DEB's hands and pulls her close.)

WIN: Scream if you don't want it.

DEB: I'm not going to scream—

WIN: Because you want me—

DEB: Because I don't want to ruin my dinner party.

WIN: I've already ruined it...and it's just a barbecue—
(*He kisses her forcefully.*) Go ahead. Scream if that wasn't
exactly—

(DEB *screams.*)

WIN: I really didn't think you'd scream. I thought you
wanted it.

DEB: I don't. You have no concept of how people feel
about you.

(DEB *looks at the house. Beat. She screams again. Everyone
rushes out of the house.*)

MIKE: Deb!

ASH: What happened?

(*They all pause.*)

MIKE: Deb—what? What's wrong.

DEB: Win...grabbed me just now and...forced me to
kiss him.

MIKE: What?

GLORY: Oh, my god.

LULU: No one ever tries to rape me— Especially not
this guy. (*She points to* ASH *and blows a raspberry.*)

MIKE: Win—

WIN: Now, Mike—

MIKE: Win, I have to fight you now.

DEB: No—

(MIKE *screams as he attacks* WIN. *The fight isn't fair at all.*
ASH, DEB *and* GLORY *are yelling for them to stop.* LULU
roots MIKE *on.* WIN *quickly gets* MIKE *to the ground and
punches him in the face two or three times before* ASH *and*
DEB *break it up.*)

WIN: Man, you made me do that!

DEB: You made him do that you dick hole!

(MIKE *stands.*)

ASH: That was very violent.

DEB: Honey—

MIKE: I'm O K.

DEB: Mike—

(MIKE *sits, in pain.*)

MIKE: No. Stop. What—Deb, tell me what happened.

WIN: Screw this.

GLORY: No, screw you WIN! What is wrong with you?! I thought we were…I thought we were good—

WIN: We are. You're the best thing I've ever had. Really. I've just always…you know…I've always had a raging boner for Deb.

LULU: I like boners.

MIKE: Always?

DEB: He's been harassing me for a while…

MIKE: How long?

DEB: Ten years?

WIN: That sounds right.

MIKE: God, I wish I'd known that before I tried to fight you.

WIN: Why?

MIKE: Because now I have to fight you again.

WIN: Oh, Mike—

MIKE: Maybe I won't. *(Pause)* Oh, fuck it.

(MIKE *attacks* WIN *again and is again quickly dispatched.* WIN *is a little more gentle this time.*)

MIKE: O K! O K! Damn it! I wish I could have hit you once. This has been—

(DEB *tries to help* MIKE.)

MIKE: No! Stop. GOD DAMN IT! I can't fight, I can't... The pride of my fucking life is a deck. How sad is that? This has been the most humiliating night of my life—

(MIKE *leans against the railing of the porch. It breaks and he falls backwards off the porch. Everyone is shocked.* DEB *and* GLORY *move to help* MIKE.)

ASH: Oh, My GOD!

(*Everyone stops.* ASH *is looking at his phone.*)

ASH: Guys...Twitter...

LULU: Two of our friends were JUST in a fight, right HERE, in front of you, in real life and you're checking Twitter?

ASH: YES, IT'S A COMPULSION! I admit it. I'm addicted, O K! But listen for a second! Um, you know earlier I said something big seemed to be happening...I think... Something... They're saying it has the potential to be a cataclysmic event.

GLORY: What?

WIN: No way.

DEB: Who is saying that?

ASH: Everybody on Twitter...and Facebook...hold on...

DEB: That's got to be a hoax.

LULU: Right? We would have known about it earlier, right?

ASH: C N N dot com has it. The President is going to speak in a minute.

(*Pause*)

DEB: I'll turn the T V on…

(They all enter the house. MIKE stands.)

MIKE: Hey, I think I hit my head…I feel sick… Where is everybody?

(MIKE struggles to get back on the porch. DEB enters from the house.)

DEB: Oh, honey. I'm sorry. I forgot—

MIKE: You forgot?

DEB: Honey, I love you.

MIKE: What's wrong?

DEB: Just come inside.

MIKE: O K. Where is everybody?

DEB: They're inside. Come in.

(DEB disappears into the house. He starts in but stops when he sees the grill. He limps to it, catches his breath and tries to light it one more time. It lights. He raises his hands in dazed triumph. Lights)

END OF ACT ONE

ACT TWO

(Lights up on the same porch, late afternoon, one year later. Camouflage netting covers half of the porch. The plants are thriving to the point of being overgrown. DEB, dressed in jeans and a worn denim shirt, is busy at a work bench. She's working with some duct tape and an empty two or three liter bottle of Coca Cola. She works in silence for a while then... We hear a wild animal scream and a loud commotion. Pause. Again. Then...)

MIKE: Son of a damn bitch!

DEB: What? What's wrong!?

(MIKE enters with a knife.)

MIKE: Dinner doesn't want to die.

DEB: I thought you said he didn't have rabies.

MIKE: Well, apparently even raccoons without rabies are bastards when you try to kill them.

DEB: Did you try stabbing him?

MIKE: No, Deb. I tried to reach in the cage and strangle him but the giant knife in my hand made it difficult.

DEB: Lemme see the knife. Lemme... They'll be here any time and dinner's not dead- Here—

(DEB goes to take the knife from MIKE.)

MIKE: Don't—

DEB: Here—

MIKE: Ah, no, This—

DEB: No—

MIKE: Wrestling for knives—

DEB: Mike, you—

MIKE: —is not safe!

(DEB *manages to get the knife and exits into the yard.*)

MIKE: Jinkies. (*To* DEB *who is off*) He's not a possum! He's not just gonna lie there. You know, they won't care if they have to wait. They'll just be happy to have meat and a story.

(*We hear the raccoon go crazy again. Beat, then* DEB *comes back on.*)

DEB: I'll get the spear.

MIKE: (*Gingerly lifting the pistol*) Why don't we use this?

DEB: I don't know if the suppressor will be quiet enough yet. It's just a prototype. You know, fire a gun, good people go away—

MIKE: Bad people try to come take your gun and probably eat you.

DEB: Right. Although, being eaten might not be that bad...

MIKE: O-ho!..Using the very real threat of cannibalism as oral sex invite. I like it. Well, baby...if we can get our hands on some soap you might find out. (*Beat*) What it's like to be eaten...by me...sexually—

DEB: Where'd you put the spear?

MIKE: Broom closet.

DEB: Look at you putting things where they go.

MIKE: I'm all grown up.

(DEB *hands* MIKE *the knife.*)

DEB: Here. I love you, honey. I'm really looking forward to this barbecue.

MIKE: Me, too. It's our one year post-apocalypsiversary.

(DEB *and* MIKE *kiss.*)

DEB: It's hard to remember anything from our pre-apocalyptic world.

MIKE: I like that. Lights up on a pre-apocalyptic world. I'll use it in tonight's story.

DEB: I wrote something!

MIKE: Uh, huh. I have roles for Glory.

DEB: She'll LOVE that!

MIKE: Yep.

DEB: Wait…What was I doing?

MIKE: Spear. Raccoon.

DEB: Right!

(DEB *goes into the house.* MIKE *puts the knife down, picks up a watering can and goes to fuss with the plants.*)

MIKE: Hello, Mister Goosefoot. How are you? Oh, that's good to hear. Do you like when I talk to you? You do? Wanna hear a story? O K. A woman's garden is growing beautifully but the darn tomatoes won't ripen. She's sick of it.

(WIN *enters and sneaks up onto the porch during* MIKE's *story. He's in a daze and completely disheveled. Dirty bathrobe, his Aviators have a lens missing, etc. He notices* MIKE, *then* MIKE's *knife. He picks up the knife as he sneaks closer.*)

MIKE: So, she goes to her neighbor and says, "Your tomatoes are ripe, mine are green. What can I do about it?" The neighbor says, "After dark go out into your garden and take all your clothes off. Tomatoes can see in the dark so they'll be embarrassed and blush. In the morning they'll all be red." Well, what the hell? She does it. The next day the neighbor asks how it worked. "So-so," she says, "The tomatoes are still green but the cucumbers are all four inches longer." That's kind of a gardening, slash, dick joke. *(Without turning)* Hey, Win. You gonna cut my throat and take everything I own?

WIN: I…was thinking about it.

MIKE: Where's Glory?

WIN: Not coming.

MIKE: You didn't eat her did you?

WIN: No. She's sick.

MIKE: Oh, no. Is she O K?

WIN: Yeah. Just didn't feel like making the long walk.

MIKE: Yeah. It sucks. We'll send a doggy bag back with you, which this time I'm happy to say is just a figure of speech.

WIN: That poor dog.

MIKE: Yeah.

WIN: I sometimes think he was the lucky one.

MIKE: The dog we ate? The dog we ate is the lucky one?

WIN: *(He starts crying.)* Yeah.

MIKE: Uh, huh. I wish you guys would move closer. Ash and Lulu did. They're in the neighborhood two blocks south. Living in the library.

WIN: We should. We should move…I just don't wanna give up the loft, I guess. *(He puts the knife down.)*

MIKE: So, society has broken down. We're part of the whatever percent left and you're still into granite counter tops.

WIN: And stainless steel appliances that don't work. *(Crying again)* That's part of the cruel joke of it all.

MIKE: Are you O K?

WIN: What do you mean?

MIKE: You're crying a little more than usual.

WIN: Yeah…

MIKE: You guys eating O K?

WIN: Yeah.

MIKE: Oh! Taters! Here. (*He grabs a towel and jumps off the porch where there are a row of old tires filled with dirt. He digs in the dirt and pulls out several potatoes and places them on the towel.*) Deb made potatoes for tonight and we wanted to send some home with you guys.

WIN: No—

MIKE: We've got plenty.

WIN: How did you figure out how to do this?

MIKE: Deb. And she designed our trap out back, where we get most of our meat. She's got us collecting rain and growing potatoes in old tires. It's funny the things you can do when you have to.

WIN: Yeah. It's funny all right. Sometimes I just laugh and laugh until my throat is raw and bloody.

MIKE: I'd make you tell me what's bothering you be but we're both men…so…Here. I'll put these inside. Just remember them when you leave.

(*DEB enters from the house with the "spear". It's a broom with a sharpened handle. She hustles past MIKE and WIN and off.*)

DEB: Hello, Win! Can't talk. I have ten minutes to murder and butcher this fucking raccoon. (*She's gone.*)

WIN: Raccoon?

MIKE: Tonight we eat like kings. Really poor kings that will eat anything. Oh! Drinks! We can get drunk tonight. Deb made a still.

WIN: Like, alcohol?

MIKE: We've got potato vodka.

WIN: She's like McGuyver with tits.

MIKE: Yes she is. It tastes like burning but it'll do the trick.

(MIKE *goes inside. We hear the dying scream of the raccoon. Beat.* DEB *enters carrying a dead raccoon on the end of her spear. She stops.*)

DEB: Where's Glory?

WIN: Not here.

DEB: You didn't eat her did you?

WIN: No.

DEB: Good. She O K?

WIN: Yes. Just a little— *(He starts crying.)* —under the weather.

DEB: Uh, huh. Did you eat her?

WIN: No! Jesus Christ!

DEB: O K. We're having raccoon and potatoes. Mike had a part for her in tonight's story.

WIN: That's…that's too bad.

DEB: It's a new one.

WIN: I'm looking forward to it.

DEB: O K. I've gotta go in and chop this little guy up.

WIN: O K.

DEB: You O K?

WIN: Yeah.

DEB: O K... *(She starts in then stops short.)* Oh, one more thing. Did you eat Glory?

WIN: No, I did not eat my girlfriend!

DEB: O K...Jeez. *(She goes inside.)*

WIN: I sold her.

(WIN sees the gun. He picks it up and contemplates shooting himself but the three liter bottle makes it really awkward. He can't figure out the right way to do it. LULUu pokes her head through the broken gate. WIN puts the gun down amongst the plants.)

LULU: *(Quietly)* Yoo-hoo. Just us. Don't spear us! Oh! Hello, Win!

(ASH follows her into the yard. They've both lost all sense of fashion. ASH is carrying a very heavy box and goes to sit it down on the table.)

ASH: Hiya, Win. Long time no see. Where's—

WIN: Glory is at home, sick. I didn't eat her.

(ASH laughs.)

LULU: Well, O K! Good to know! Where are the hosts?

WIN: Inside.

(LULU opens the back door.)

LULU: Helloooo. We're here! Don't spear us.

DEB: *(From inside)* Come in! I'm skinning dinner.

LULU: My god, I love what you've done with the place. Is that a still? *(She goes into the house.)*

ASH: Check this out. You're gonna like this. *(He takes out a ham radio wired to a car battery...or something to provide power.)*

WIN: That's like a C B, right?

ASH: It's a ham radio. Top of the line. Internal antenna. This thing cost five thousand dollars when there was money.

WIN: Where did you get it?

ASH: The mall. Everything had either been stolen, probably the first week, or busted. I mean some people really messed this mall up. These people hated Ralph Lauren. But anyway, in Radio Shack, which was totally ransacked, this thing was just sitting there, untouched. Like someone had left it for me.

WIN: Have you heard other people?

ASH: I just got it up yesterday but yeah. I have. Just a couple of times. I'm just listening right now. Low profile. I think one of the conversations I picked up was…the people were not nice, I think. We have to be careful. Not everyone left is civilized.

(DEB, MIKE *and* LULU *enter.*)

LULU: God, the smell of a rodent's blood makes me horny.

ASH: *(To* WIN*)* See?

(DEB *has a tray of raccoon steaks and potatoes,* MIKE *has a tray of glasses full of clear alcohol and a pitcher of tomato juice.)*

DEB: Is a raccoon a rodent?

MIKE: I don't know.

ASH: *(Reaching for his pocket)* I'll Goog… Hmm. *(He goes back to the radio.)*

LULU: You've heard of amputees who swear that the limb they've lost itches? A year later, Ash still has phantom phone.

ASH: *(To the group)* Guys. Listen to this… He starts tuning the radio.

LULU: Oh, his new I-Phone.

ASH: The library is my new I-Phone.

LULU: Same thing.

ASH: This is communication. My I-Phone was for gathering information, like the library.

LULU: His phone wasn't for communication.

ASH: I never called anyone. Shut it. Now, this lady is a recorded message that plays on a loop. (*He turns the radio up.*)

FEMALE VOICE 1: …a short inhale of breath as his hand brushed her thigh. He was emboldened to explore further. To push his boundaries as he pushed her skirt, up, up until she could feel a breeze touching her most private region, her vulva…

(ASH *turns the radio down.*)

ASH: You get the point.

DEB: It's porn.

ASH: It's erotica.

MIKE: It's really shitty erotica.

ASH: I wouldn't have used "Vulva".

MIKE: Right.

LULU: It was doing the trick for me.

ASH: What I find fascinating is this. We were just nearly wiped out as a species. Right? As far as technology goes we've been set back what, a thousand years? And the last remnants of the technology we have left are pieces like this. And we, as humans, feel compelled to put porn on it. Right away.

LULU: We listened to it last night and humped like wildebeests.

ASH: We did.

MIKE: …All right. I'll fire up the grill. *(He starts it up without even thinking.)*

LULU: Oh! We brought a gift!

DEB: You shouldn't have.

LULU: Deb. Please. *(She goes to the box* ASH *brought.)* O K, so we've been eating shit for the last year. Well, not literally, but we did drink pee one time.

ASH: We don't recommend it.

LULU: Yeah, it is technically organic, but no, we can't recommend it.

ASH: No.

LULU: It sucks. Anyway, we've been eating a lot of squab lately—

ASH: Pigeons. We open all the top floor windows of the library. They wander in—

LULU: And we rip their little heads off. So, here… two pigeons for Mike and Deb. And two for Win and Glory.

*(*LULU *hands out the pigeons gift wrapped in newspaper.)*

MIKE: Nice!

DEB: Thank you!

WIN: Thanks—

*(*LULU *takes out two clear seasoning containers.)*

LULU: And try seasoning it with a little soap scum.

DEB: Soap scum?

LULU: Uh, huh.

MIKE: I'm not going to do that.

LULU: Yeah. I know. That's what we thought. But it's imminently more palatable than the soap was.

Reminds me of ginger. You know, you've seen Chaplin eat that shoe? You're like, oh, funny.

ASH: Very comical.

LULU: Right. Very comical. But it's not funny when you're the one eating the shoe.

MIKE: You ate a shoe?

LULU: I tried. And I almost choked it down. Thanks to this stuff.

(LULU *hands out small, clear seasoning jars full of soap scum. They have little ribbons tied to them.*)

DEB: Thanks you guys. This is so thoughtful.

LULU: Well, it's the least we could do.

ASH: We would have starved to death without you guys. You figured out apocalypse living pretty fast.

DEB: Well, I lost those last ten vanity pounds but, yeah.

MIKE: It's Deb. She's the hunter and the gatherer.

DEB: Well, having a fenced in back yard was important. So, we could hide our little garden back here. And the garden was drawing critters and we figured out how to trap them and voila. Survival.

MIKE: It wasn't that easy. We were lucky.

DEB: Our house is so ugly we were spared the looting.

ASH: God, the looting.

DEB: People getting T Vs. It was the end of the world as we knew it and people were stealing T Vs.

MIKE: There wasn't anything good on before the apocalypse.

DEB: Right. Now, we ransacked our dead neighbors' houses—

ASH: Well, yeah.

MIKE: You had to.

LULU: Absolute necessity.

DEB: You just had to be smart about it.

LULU: Yep.

MIKE: I'm gonna go ahead and put the meat on but it'll be a little while.

ASH: Slow and low.

MIKE: You know it. Deb. Moonshine.

DEB: Yeah! Let's drink! I made potato alcohol. It's vodka-esque. It's good for washing out wounds and getting you fuucked uup.

(ASH *laughs out loud and then says:*)

ASH: L O L.

DEB: This is crushed tomatoes. Bloody Marys anyone?

(*They all cheer.* DEB *starts pouring.*)

LULU: *(Pointedly)* Virgin for me.

DEB: What?

LULU: No alcohol for me.

MIKE: Are we on the wagon?

LULU: Nope. We're pregnant! Ahh!!!

DEB: Wow!

MIKE: Oh, shit!

LULU: I know! It's awesome!

MIKE: No, I meant, "Oh shit!" Like, "Oh, shit!"

DEB: No—

ASH: We can do it. I've been studying. I will deliver my own child.

MIKE: That's quite a pronouncement.

ASH: Well, I will. I think I can do it.

MIKE: You have to. No other choice.

ASH: Right.

MIKE: But still, it's scary.

ASH: Yeah.

MIKE: I mean being a parent is frightening enough.

ASH: Yep.

MIKE: But to be responsible for the health of mother and baby at such a delicate…with absolutely no experience.

ASH: Uh, huh.

DEB: Mike. Are you an idiot? You're scaring them.

LULU: We're not scared.

ASH: I'm scared. I am really scared.

LULU: Honey.

ASH: Even if I could just have ten minutes with Google Health.

DEB: You don't need Google.

ASH: I do. I picture myself alone—

LULU: I'll be there—

ASH: —the baby is turned the wrong way and with the cord thing wrapped around its neck and I have to give you a C-Section with my teeth.

LULU: Just use a knife!

ASH: I don't picture having a knife!

LULU: Why are you picturing this?

ASH: I don't know! This pregnancy is like a waking nightmare! *(Pause)* I mean, it's a joyous and amazing gift…that I have an overwhelming sense of impending doom about. That's all.

(LULU blows a raspberry at him.)

DEB: I think it's awesome and just let us know if you need help.

LULU: We were going to ask…

DEB: We'll be there.

LULU: I love you, Deb. We love you guys.

DEB: We love you, too. So, what…how did it happen?

LULU: Ha!

MIKE: Yeah, what position were you in?

DEB: I will stab you with the mop. I just—were you trying?

LULU: No. Oh, no, no, no, no. We were using the rhythm method and Ash has no rhythm—

ASH: Nope.

LULU: And the funny thing is that before…before, you know, the end of the world we never did it—

ASH: Never—

LULU: I would go to bed drunk—

ASH: Always—

LULU: Always—

ASH: Always—

LULU: —and, right, I said always, and he would stay up on his computer, reading Scandinavian design blogs—

ASH: *(Pining)* Yeah—

LULU: Then, you know how if someone asked you what you would do if you knew it was your last day on earth you'd say…?

WIN: Screw.

LULU: Right…so I guess we just always felt like it was our last day on earth so we've been screwing—

ASH: Non-stop.

DEB: That's so beautiful.

MIKE: Is it?

ASH: And at one point we didn't bathe for a month.

LULU: It was like Mutual of Omaha's Wild Kingdom—

DEB: Alright.

LULU: We were like wildebeests.

(ASH *and* LULU *make wildebeest noises at each other. An inside joke*)

MIKE: That's your second sexual mention of wildebeests.

LULU: Yeah, yeah. And now we're preggo!

DEB: Yay! Hey, hey, hey, a toast. Get your terrible alcohol. To Lulu and Ash and to the little wildebeest baby they're gonna have. And, to…to us all. I know…I know I haven't shaved my armpits in a year and, and I know I could get an infection tomorrow and die…but there's not another group of people on Earth I'd rather live through the apocalypse with. Even if there was another group of people on earth.

ASH: Hear, hear.

(*They drink. It's not good.*)

ASH: Chunky.

(*It's terrible but they drink again.*)

WIN: (*To* ASH *and* LULU) Aren't you guys worried about SIDS?

DEB: Really?

MIKE: Win, you are such and Eyeore.

WIN: Yeah. I suppose I am.

(*The radio comes to life. They gather around it slowly as they listen.*)

FEMALE VOICE 2: Hello. My name is Sarah Martin—

ASH: The hell?

FEMALE VOICE 2: —communications director for the Northern Louisiana Principality. If anyone is listening, this message is an invitation. As far as we know we're the largest settlement in what was the United States. We've been growing steadily over the last year and we're…well, we're a small town. We are civilized and peaceful. We have clean water and are working every day towards renewable food sources, and have limited electricity. We need workers, citizens to aid our development. We need people willing to sacrifice for the common good. We offer protection, fellowship, and a new society to anyone hearing this who's willing to abide by the rule of law. We're located on County Road 3194, three miles East of LA 1 in a town that used to be Vivian, Louisiana. This message will repeat again in five minutes. If you'd like to make contact with us turn to channel 159. Godspeed.

DEB: Oh, my god.

LULU: I don't want to live in Louisiana.

DEB: I don't— What are you doing?

ASH: Turning to channel 159?

MIKE: No.

DEB: Yeah, yeah, no. No. Let's talk about it.

ASH: What? It's people! Nice people!

LULU: We don't have to tell them where we are.

DEB: We won't.

ASH: What does it hurt to talk to them? I'm sorry. I don't get it—

DEB: We just need to discuss—

ASH: It's people. It's stuff. They have food and water.

DEB: They say they have food and water—

ASH: You don't trust it—

DEB: I don't know these people. I know you guys. I trust you.

LULU: Right. So, we talk to them then decide whether they're O K.

DEB: We won't be able to tell. We can't risk it.

LULU: Mike?

MIKE: There wouldn't…there wouldn't be a way to really tell if they're on the level.

LULU: Where's Win?

WIN: I'm right here.

LULU: Oh. I forget you're around sometimes. No offense.

WIN: None taken.

LULU: What do you think about this?

WIN: Deliverance was set in Louisiana.

MIKE: That's something to chew on.

DEB: It was set in Georgia.

MIKE: Right.

WIN: Louisiana is worse.

MIKE: True.

ASH: Which of us three would get raped?

WIN: Mike is Burt Reynolds. You're the other guy and…I'm piggy. I'm the piggy.

MIKE: I worry about you.

WIN: Nobody loves the piggy.

ASH: I always assumed I'd be the piggy.

MIKE: I'm pretty happy with Burt Reynolds.

ASH: Yeah. That's great.

LULU: Guys! None of you are Burt Reynolds! *(Beat)* Deb is Burt Reynolds. Everybody, let's discuss this!

DEB: We are.

LULU: Let's discuss it more! Until we decide I'm right! People. Other humans. A town! Let's sit. Sit. Let's shoot the bull. Tonight we eat. We'll be entertained and, I guess we make a huge decision about this bitch from Louisiana.

(Everybody sits except WIN *who hovers to the side. Beat)*

ASH: It doesn't make sense to not at least talk to them. They won't know where we are. I could just switch right over—

DEB: No, goddammit!

ASH: Whoa.

DEB: Sorry. Sorry. Look, we have to be smart about this.

LULU: We will.

DEB: It's not a glib thing, to just, just—

LULU: It's not glib. It's not. I understand that they could be Louisiana butt rapists.

DEB: Or worse—

MIKE: There's nothing worse—

ASH: They have electricity! Electricity!

LULU: I wanna eat some ice cream!

ASH: Computers—

DEB: Stop—

LULU: Food processors—

ASH: Sonic-care toothbrushes—

DEB: God—

LULU: Blenders—

ASH: Espresso machines—

LULU: Sex toys that you plug into the wall—

WIN: They'll trick us, guys! They'll trick us. They'll
tell us—Lulu—Lulu, they'll tell us they have dildos
that you plug into the wall if that's what you want to
hear. They'll take us in and talk to us about…about
survival and then they'll take the only thing that we've
ever had that has been real, that's been important, the
only thing we've ever truly earned. They'll leave us
broken. Everything we thought about ourselves before
the apocalypse was all wrong. Then just as we were
coming to terms with who we thought we were now…
it'll just get ripped away from us again. I'm not sure
we'll have anything to live for.
The darkness that has been outside will finally swallow
us. The darkness that we used to keep at bay with
money, and sex, and pride, and…and feeling big,
feeling strong, feeling successful, and cars, and where
we lived, and how much better we were doing than
the people we measured ourselves against. (Gestures to
MIKE) Now we only have candles and our wits. Both
so easily snuffed. Make no mistake, the darkness will
wash over us, inky, black, choking…It will be the…
true end of us.

(Beat)

MIKE: So, Win, is that a nay or…?

WIN: Nay.

MIKE: Win's a nay. Deb's a nay and I am, too, I think
so—

ASH: It's mine. It's my radio. So…so I'll just do it when
we take it home and..and not mention you—

DEB: No. No you don't—

ASH: I can if I want to.

DEB: What?

ASH: I can do what I want.

DEB: No, you can't—

LULU: Deb—

DEB: We voted!

ASH: It's my property—

(DEB *knocks* ASH *away and straddles the radio. She holds a knife above it, with both hands on the hilt of the knife, as if to stab the radio.*)

DEB: No— No you don't— Not with my life! I will—I will destroy your technology!

ASH: Deb—

DEB: Don't…don't you like what we have here? Don't you like it? How slow and deliberate it is? Think. Think about what we have! We have our own society. Our own rules. Our own ideas of what we need. Haven't we— Haven't Mike and I done enough for you—

LULU: Deb, this is crazy—

DEB: I know—

MIKE: It is, honey—

DEB: Mike. Mike tell them. Please tell them— tell us. Tell us—tell them what we have here. Why you are afraid— We've talked— We've talked about something just—just like this. You were honest with me. Be honest with them.

MIKE: I'm—I am torn, honey.

DEB: C'mon. I'm squatting over this thing. My quads can't take it. Say the really honest shit you were saying to me! C'mon—

MIKE: I kind of like my life right now. I love my life, actually. Don't you guys, a little bit? I mean, I have friends who I can trust. And it seems…selfish…I'm the last contemporary writer…I have no competition so it's almost like I'm pretty good.

LULU: You are really good—

DEB: Amazing—

ASH: You make me wonder sometimes what it must be like to have an imagination.

MIKE: See. I'm…useful. You guys come here clamoring for a story…and food, but also a story. My story. To see what I've come up with. To escape for a while…Even when we all thought we were going to die. Especially then.

WIN: You helped us think about something other than our impending deaths.

LULU: Yeah—

DEB: Yes—

MIKE: Jesus. I'm actually, truly useful as an artist. Really. An artist. And that's really weird but it feels really good. For me and all the other artists if there are any. So, that's what I've got. I'm scared, I guess that I'll lose that. And you all.

DEB: I take care of all of you like I used to take care of just Mike. And he was harder to take care of because his needs were all emotional and kind of girly—

MIKE: All right—

DEB: —and that's just, almost impossible. But I took care of us.

WIN: It's true. I would have died.

MIKE: Me too.

DEB: *(She sits down.)* And I guess, I'm just a little too proud of that.

LULU: No. No. You're fine. You're— It's— *(Looking at* ASH.*)* We do have a lot more fun now.

ASH: So much sex.

LULU: He puts it absolutely everywhere.

ASH: Oh, yeah.

*(*ASH *and* LULU *look at each other lovingly. Sincerely)*

LULU: He used to be like, "Ewww. Poop comes out of there." Then at some point he stopped caring about that.

ASH: Yeah, that just doesn't seem to matter anymore.

DEB: O K... So, what if it is civilization? What if it is safe...and easy? Who will we become?

LULU: Food and shelter and safety...and love. Those are my only worries now. They seem...I don't know...

ASH: They seem more natural.

DEB: Right. So...Nay?

*(*ASH *and* LULU *together)*

ASH: Nay.

LULU: Nay. *(She rises and puts the knife away.)*

WIN: But what if they have an O B/G Y N? For the baby.

DEB: Oh, shit. Never mind. Yay.

MIKE: Yeah. Yay.

LULU: Yay. We gotta see.

MIKE: Man, for a post-apocalyptic world we handle conflict pretty well.

ASH: We really do.

LULU: And I really feel like I learned something.

DEB: Well...I was going to stab the radio.

(Everybody but WIN *thinks this is funny.)*

DEB: I jumped on it and…and was gonna stab it. I really was.

LULU: That was crazy—

MIKE: You looked like a monkey—

DEB: A monkey? No!

LULU: It was ape-like.

*(*JOHN, *a tall, bearded man in a flannel shirt sticks his head through the gate.)*

JOHN: Howdy, folks. Don't shoot me.

(The group is startled.)

JOHN: Whoa! Whoa! You are jumpy! Hey, it's O K. It's O K. Can…can I come up on the porch there? O K. O K. Everybody relax. How is everybody today? *(Silence)* O K. So…excuse me but I was listening in to make sure I was at the right place, so… You folks were talking about the new age we find ourselves in. I'm gonna sit down now if that's O K? O K. *(He sits. He's calm and still throughout.)* Oh, that's nice. Now when I sit I actually appreciate it. I used to sit all the time. I sat at work at a desk. I sat at home in front of the T V. It was so easy. I wanted more, though, stuff I couldn't have. My heart was restless but my body didn't move. Then everything went right to hell, didn't it? I had to stand up. And I liked that feeling, I don't know about you folks. I liked moving around and needing something. Needing something so bad, something so necessary, so primal, that I just had to have it. There were no other options. Am I right? You folks went through it. You do it, you find it, you take it or you die. Right? It was refreshing. Am I right? *(Silence)* You are some chatty sons of bitches. I had something to do: stay alive. And it suited me, I guess, cuz I'm still doing it. This may be the longest I've sat still in…months. No,

I'm always moving now. Always hunting. Can I be
honest with you all? I think I can. Cuz I know Win
here and he told me all about you, except where you
were. Friends taking care of each other. It's nice. You
remind me of me and my friends a little. Lemme tell
you a story. A short story. I had fallen in with these
folks in Atlanta, or outside of Atlanta. Four of us guys;
Me, Jim, Ted, Michael, all looking out for each other.
Buddies. God, Ted was funny as hell. Even in the face
of all this. Always good for...for a laugh. Man, I loved
Ted. Anyway, we were traveling and following every
rumor about safe places and...we were dying. We
were wasting away. And I was in my sleeping bag one
night. Looking up at the sky and figuring it was my
last night to see it. And...I was thinking back to the
man I was before...Always wanting, but never doing
anything about it...and then I looked at my situation,
dying, scared, hungry. And then I was truthful to
myself, about myself for the first time. I figured out
who I really was and how I fit into this world. That's
real happiness. I just stood right up and I put my hand
over Ted's mouth and I stuck my knife right into his
neck. And it worked like that for the others, too. Their
eyes went wide then just out. In two minutes I was
alone. *(He takes a gun out of his pants and places it on the
table.)* Then I took everything they had that I needed.
It hadn't been enough for the four of us. But it was
enough for me. Your friend here, Win...he's kind of a
douche bag. You probably all know that, right?

(General agreement)

JOHN: I came across him and that sweet, sweet...Glory.
Perfect name. And she had something I needed. I could
see they were both as soft as tissue paper but he let me
know that he was a business man and wanted to make
a deal. So, I made him a couple of offers. I wouldn't kill

him and I get the girl. Or I could kill him and I'd get the girl. He jumped at that first one.

So, I walked outta there with a real woman. Neither would tell me where you all were. So, I just followed his dumbass over here. And low and behold…two more women. An embarrassment of riches. O K? Everybody understand the situation? I'm going to kill you fellas. Sorry, I don't need you. Then me and the ladies will take all your nice stuff, load it into my van out front and split. *(Pause)* Well…I guess we've talked enou—

(JOHN stands up with his gun. In one quick motion, WIN spins, quick draws the pistol out of the plants where it was left earlier in the act, and shoots John in the head. He's dead. Blood splatters the side of the house. Long Silence… then:)

DEB: The silencer works.

(Beat)

ASH: *(To WIN)* That was very impressive.

DEB: We'll talk more about Louisiana tomorrow. I'm gonna check the van for Glory. Was it just him, Win?

(WIN nods.)

ASH: I'll come for back up.

LULU: Me three!

(They start inside.)

LULU: Do you have an extra spear?

(They're gone. Silence)

MIKE: Oh, raccoon! He goes to the grill and turns the pieces of raccoon.) Hey, nice timing. Good amount of char. I'm getting pretty good at this. Raccoon, the other red meat. Raccoon, The San Francisco treat. Plop, Plop, Fizz, Fizz, oh what a Raccoon it is. God, I miss commercials. *(Pause. He is busy.)* Thanks for not telling him where we were.

WIN: Yeah.

MIKE: And thanks for blowing his head off. That was pretty cool, too.

WIN: Anytime.

MIKE: It was, like, practiced and professional looking.

WIN: I've never shot a gun before. I used to do this a lot during meetings. *(He does "double finger guns".)* I guess it's pretty much the same thing.

(DEB leads GLORY out of the house. ASH and LULU follow.)

MIKE: Glory, you O K?

GLORY: Yeah, thanks, Mark. I'm O K.

DEB: Are you sure he didn't hurt you?

GLORY: He just had me tied up while he waited on Win to leave. Thank you, Deb.

DEB: Thank, Win. He killed him.

GLORY: Really?

DEB: Yep.

GLORY: Oh, baby…

(GLORY goes to WIN.)

WIN: I'm so sorry, sugar tits…I was too scare—

(She kisses him hard.)

LULU: They still got it.

(They are all still for several moments. MIKE cooking. GLORY and WIN together. ASH and LULU have found their way to each other. DEB stares at the corpse.)

DEB: Well…Jesus. There's a dead guy here. On our deck. That's really fucked up.

(They all agree.)

DEB: What… What do we do now?

(Pause)

MIKE: Raccoon's done…

DEB: Well…I could eat.

ASH: Me too.

LULU: Me three.

DEB: Oh, what time is it?

LULU: Six-ish.

DEB: Story time…

LULU: Oooh! Dinner theater.

(They look at each other, deciding.)

DEB: Dinner theater. Let's do it!

ASH: Awesome.

GLORY: Yes!

LULU: Honey, help me with the dead guy, please.

ASH: You're not lifting the corpse. You're pregnant.

LULU: I'm not that pregnant.

DEB: *(Getting* GLORY *comfortable)* You're pregnant enough to not lift a big dead guy. Mike, help Ash. Lift with your legs. And there's some brain or something on the door.

LULU: I got it. *(She gets a rag and cleans up the blood and brains.)*

MIKE: Okeedokee. Deb, will you pull the raccoon off?

DEB: Oh, food and a story is exactly what I need right now.

*(*DEB *starts taking the food off of the grill.* ASH *and* MIKE *lift the corpse.)*

WIN: I'm so sorry. I was a coward earlier.

GLORY: You just didn't know your character yet. Everything that is unattainable for us now will one day be near and clear... But we must work.

WIN: Wow.

(They hug.)

GLORY: It's from a play.

DEB: Story time! We'll lose the light.

(ASH and MIKE toss the corpse off of the porch in the same place where MIKE fell in the first act.)

MIKE: Glory, you have a role this time. Or roles. You'll play all of the women.

GLORY: Character work! I love it.

MIKE: I've underlined your parts. Each , except the mom, is described a little in the prose before they speak. She's just kind of a mom. Sorry to spring it on you.

GLORY: I love cold reading. It's like an audition.

MIKE: You'll do great.

GLORY: *(Looking at the script)* Yeah. Oh, yeah I'm gonna rock this.

DEB: *(Handing ASH and LULU plates)* Dinner is served.

LULU: Yum!

MIKE: It needs to rest.

DEB: We know, honey. Ash—

ASH: Thank you, so much—

MIKE: O K. There's a mom, a crazy lady—

GLORY: —Love it—

MIKE: A judge, annndd...that's it. I'll narrate and play the main guy.

GLORY: Got it.

(DEB *has made* WIN *a plate. She hands it to him and then grabs a plate for herself.* ASH, DEB, *and* LULU *settle in chairs facing* GLORY *and* MIKE.)

MIKE: O K. Ready. *(Reading)* Once upon a time—

LULU: I love the "once upon a time" ones—

ASH: Shhh…

MIKE: Once upon a time, in a pre-apocalyptic world, there was a little boy named Max whose mother loved him very, very much.

GLORY: You are my sweet little child.

MIKE: His mother would coo at him.

GLORY: My sweetest little thing.

LULU: Awwe..

ASH: Shh—

MIKE: Then, unfortunately, Max hit puberty.

GLORY: What are you doing in that bathroom!?

MIKE: I'm combing my hair, mom!

GLORY: Oy vey! How much can one boy comb his hair?

MIKE: And so Max was no longer her sweetest little thing. But she loved him still. Sure, he felt shame about his nearly constant, vigorous hair combing. But he realized that he was who he was. His hair needed combing, he had no clue how to get someone to comb it for him, and it wasn't going to comb itself *(except sometimes at night)*. But then…then at the end of the his eighth grade school year, Becky Amundsen moved in next door.

GLORY: *(As Becky)* Hey.

MIKE: *(As Max)* Hey.
What followed was a classic, but true summer of young love.

(The lights begin to fade.)

MIKE: It was a perfect season for two fourteen year olds, together, with nothing else to do but discover each other. That is, until Becky disappeared…

LULU: Uh ohhh…

ASH: Shhh…

(Lights out)

END OF PLAY